The Vocabulary
of the
Seelenkalender

The Vocabulary of the *Seelenkalender*

A German-English Glossary of Rudolf Steiner's *Calendar of the Soul*

Compiled by
David Eyes

*Including Rudolf Steiner's original German text
and an English verse translation by Ernst Lehrs*

BLTC Press
Santa Cruz

The Vocabulary of the Seelenkalender

Introduction, Glossaries, and special contents of this edition are Copyright © 2024 by David Eyes

Original German language text of the *Seelenkalender* verses by Rudolf Steiner were a section of *Kalendar* published in 1912 by Philosophisch-Theosophischer Verlag, Berlin, 1912. This content is in the public domain.

English verse translation by Ernst Lehrs of the *Calendar of the Soul* Copyright © 1963 by Rudolf Steiner Press, used by permission

Published by BLTC Press
Santa Cruz, CA
www.bltcpress.com

ISBN 978-1-60551-304-1

R2

With thanks to my earliest teachers of German: EMG, and my teachers of almost fifty years ago at Drew University. Thanks also to Susanna Gaertner for her support.

Particular thanks to my wife, Marije Miller, who not only supports my projects with love and advice, but also tolerates my butchering of her native Dutch when I attempt it, always with my (rather bad in itself) German "accent" mixed in.

Corrections and suggestions for future editions are quite welcome, with the reminder that the goal is not to read into the Glossary a given "correct" sense of the *Seelenkalender*, but simply to point the German-naive reader towards their own further study. Send such notices to: seelenkalender@bltcpress.com

About this work

Among anthroposophists, the *Calendar of the Soul* is perhaps one of the most broadly read of Rudolf Steiner's works. A reading of the current week's verse is often a meditative preliminary to a gathering of anthroposophists. It is certainly the most translated of Steiner's works; there are even compendiums of translations. Studying these many different translations, one quickly sees that there are many nuances of meaning found in the German verses. If one has a smattering of knowledge of German, one can soon sense a deeper connection to the original by noting differences in word choice, rhythm, tone, word order, and so on between translations and referring back to the original. My own ability to appreciate the original — being myself only a partially literate reader of German — has been greatly enriched by seeing how different translators have approached the task, often with different priorities in mind.

English editions of the *Calendar of the Soul* invariably include the original German, and one may often hear it spoken aloud in circles where German speakers are available. For many reasons, including its brevity and simplicity as compared with a long-form lecture or writing by Steiner, it seems a natural place to begin if one wishes to acquaint oneself with Steiner in his original German.

For a number of years, I have felt the impulse to create a work such as this, having observed that the German vocabulary of the *Seelenkalender* is reasonably finite — around 500 unique words if you take account of variations due to case, tense, or conjugation. Quite a number of these unique words are themselves compounded of often repeated constituent words, reducing again the actual vocabulary knowledge needed to begin to appreciate the text with comprehension. For example, the German *welt* (world) occurs no less than 53 times, often in compounds such as *Weltenlicht* (world light) and *Weltenworte* (world-word), whose headwords — *licht* (light) and *worte* (word) themselves also appear repeatedly. This work was undertaken as much for purposes of my own study as for the study of others. It is offered here in mindfulness of its limitations as a first effort in this direction.

The book is presented in two ways.

The first part of the book is arranged as if the text were to be studied in a linear fashion, from the first verse through the last. As the German text is presented, if a word is being introduced for the first time, it is italicized. Looking at verse 12, for example:

Und bin ich in den Sinneshöhen,
So flammt in meinen Seelentiefen
Aus Geistes *Feuerwehen*
Der Götter *Wahrheitswort*:
In *Geistesgründen* suche *ahnend*
Dich *geistverwandt* zu finden.

The words rendered in a Roman font have been introduced somewhere in the previous verses. On the page opposite the verse itself, you will find all of the new, italicized words defined in English (*bin, Sinneshöhen, flammt,* etc.). While the German word when first listed is rerpresented as it appears in the facing verse, the definition provided may also apply to alternative inflections, cases, or parts of speech if the word appears elsewhere in such a different form. These other forms are listed together in glossary.

Although new words are introduced and defined throughout, one will soon discover that a good number of the "new" words are compounded of words previously encountered. Although in this example, *Sinneshöhen* is newly introduced, *sinn* (sense) appears for the first time in verse 2 in the word *Sinnesalls* (senses-all). *Geist* (spirit), found here in *Geistesgründen* and *geistverwandt*, (spirit grounds and spirit kindred) will have appeared already four previous times.

The definitions are listed in the order in which the words appear in the corresponding verse.

An English verse translation is also provided for general reference at the bottom of the same page as the German verse.

In the second part of the book, an alphabetically organized complete glossary is provided, with the definition for each word as well as a cross-reference to the verse numbers where the word is found. If different forms of the same root word are found in the verses, these different forms are listed together.

About the English Verse Translation

The included translation is by Ernst Lehrs, a pupil of Rudolf Steiner. Lehrs was born in Germany and lived for many years in the UK as a Waldorf teacher.

Although his translation is in many ways straightforward, its inclusion is not meant to suggest that it is in any way more correct than others. It is best to think of the translation verses as one *possible* version, provided to aid your own developing comprehension of the German text while you work through it directly. You should quickly see that as you begin to grasp the vocabulary, whole lines may be placed in different order in the translation, and so on. In part Lehrs is simply accommodating the differences in German grammar and sentence structure or, in some cases, intending a literary effect deemed more suitable to the English idiom. Sometimes literary considerations will cause significant words in the original to be excluded. Note that British English spelling is used in Lehr's translation.

Some things to know about the German Language

The focus of this work is the vocabulary itself as an entry point to the text. It is not intended as a primer on German vocabulary or grammar but simply as a way to develop a connection with the original. However, a very minimal understanding German grammar is useful to avoid confusion as you begin to study the text through the vocabulary. Perhaps the most notable difference between German and English grammar are the use in German of cases, and the effect of this on both word order and word endings; this feature makes for different word-order usages than you would find in English. A further key difference is that German is a gendered language.

Nouns are either masculine, feminine, or neuter. The articles — indefinite, English "a" and definite, English "the" — each have different forms depending on the gender of the thing referenced. The German table, fork, and book — *Tisch, Gabel,* and *Buch* — are masculine, feminine, and neuter, respectively. Their corresponding articles are *der Tisch, die Gabel,* and *das Buch.* All three forms simply mean "the." Or, in the indefinite article instance, *ein Tisch, eine Gabel,* and *ein Buch.* Their association with a given gender is essentially arbitrary, having evolved out of the earliest stages of the language from similarly gendered progenitors.

German grammar, while complex, is systematic and follows specific rules. It requires that the endings of articles, pronouns, prepositions, and adjectives, agree with their respective nouns in gender, number, and case. For example, the word *klein* (small) can take three forms (in the strong declension case) depending on the affected noun: *kleiner Hund* (small dog, masculine); *kleine Katze* (small cat, feminine); *kleines Kind* (small child, neuter).

Case is a more challenging difference: nominative, accusative, dative, and genitive. These require further changes to the articles to be used and to other endings that indicate the syntactic function of a noun — as direct object, subject, indirect object, or indicating possession or origin. Depending on the case (or, syntactic function) within a sentence, the masculine definite article — *Der,* as indicated above, can alternatively take the form of *der, den, dem,* or *das.* And so on with feminine die and neuter das. (The somewhat archaic "who" and "whom" in English are examples of the same word being formed differently depending on syntactic function.)

Because of the way these articles and endings signal the grammatical function, which, in English, is primarily done by word order, patterns of word order are also sometimes quite different than in English. These details comprise a large amount of the heavy lifting in learning to read and speak German, aside from the obvious difference in vocabulary. Taking account of this further is beyond the scope of this work and left for the reader's possible general study of German. It is mentioned here largely by way of explaining that the same word stem may be encountered with different endings — and for purposes of the vocabulary here, they are listed together in providing a definition. One will have to feel one's way into the sometimes strange-seeming sentence structure of the German text. The English verse translation can serve as a partial guide here, remembering that a poetical translation of German into English will not necessarily preserve the closest rendering of the original grammatical sentence structure.

Nouns in German are capitalized. Nouns may sometimes be formed from verb forms: "*schauen*," to look or to see, has the noun form "*das Schauen*," the seeing (or gazing, beholding). In the *Seelenkalender*, both forms of the word may be found; if capitalized, it is a noun form. Also it may be helpful to observe that somewhat generally, plural forms of nouns are formed by adding -en. This is simply a hint; many words end with -en that are not plural nouns, and not all nouns ending in -en are plural (cf. *Schauen* above). Note that in the German verses, all initial words of a line are capitalized: if the word is not a noun, note that it will not be capitalized in the definition on the facing page.

There are two typographic differences from English found in the verses: the umlaut (*ä, ö, ü*) and the *scharfes s*: ß. The umlaut modifies the pronunciation of the corresponding vowel, and the *scharfes s* is a typographic convention for what would otherwise be writen as a double s.

Pronunciation of German is secondary to first deepening comprehension of the vocabulary, and beyond the scope of this volume. You may of course wish to have a sense of the mantric quality of the spoken German; one help for this is to find audio clip examples available online for individual words or phrases. There are also online services that can "read" German text aloud.

If you are already familiar with *Calendar of the Soul*, you likely have a favorite version in English translation and wish to simply use this book as an adjunct. Comparing translations always provides additional insight.

Dates

The verses are, in the first instance, intended as subject of meditation week by week. According to Steiner, the *Seelenkalender* is meant to start at Easter — which, being a movable feast, changes year to year. The question of how to adapt the sequence to a given year is considered variously by different writers.

Working with verse 1 in this way thus always begins at Easter of the current year. Specific dates are not indicated in this text, although the *Seelenkalender* is typically published with verse 1 starting on April 7, which corresponds with the date of Easter in its first year of publication, that is, for the years 1912/1913. Although the soul-processes of the *Seelenkalender* are reflected in the course of the year, they are in themselves timeless, and the sequence may be studied with profit as a cycle complete in itself.

Rudolf Steiner's Preface to the Edition of 1918

The year has a life of its own and the human soul can feel this life. If the soul is open to the influence of the year as it changes week by week, then through living with the course of the year it will truly be able to discover itself. It will feel how through this close connection forces come into existence which strengthen it from within. The soul will find that such latent forces need to be awakened through a sympathetic awareness of the significance of the progression of the world in the passing of the seasons. Only then will it begin to become aware of the delicate but significant threads between itself and the world into which it has been born.

In this calendar is given a verse for each week, through which the soul can experience what occurs during that week as a part of the whole life of the year. The verses are meant to express what can resound in the soul if it is united with this life of the year. My aim has been a healthy feeling of unity with the course of nature, from which a sound experience of self-realization can arise, for I believe that to experience the movement of the world in the sense expressed in such verses is something the soul desires, if only it can understand itself aright.

Anthroposophischer Seelenkalender

The Verses

1

Wenn aus den Weltenweiten
Die Sonne spricht zum Menschensinn
Und Freude aus den Seelentiefen
Dem Licht sich eint im Schauen,
Dann ziehen aus der Selbstheit Hülle
Gedanken in die Raumesfernen
Und binden dumpf
Des Menschen Wesen an des Geistes Sein.

When from the width of worlds
The Sun speaks to the human sense,
And joy out of the depths of soul
Unites with light in Man's beholding,
Then thoughts withdraw from Selfhood's sheath
To farthest distances of space
And dimly bind
Man's being to the Spirit's life.

wenn	if, when
aus	out
den	the (see 'things to know')
Weltenweiten	world widths
die	the (see 'things to know')
Sonne	sun
spricht	speaks
zum	to the (zu dem, zu der)
Menschensinn	human senses
und	and
Freude	joy
Seelentiefen	soul depths
dem	the (see 'things to know')
Licht	light
sich	oneself
eint	unites
im	in the (in dem)
Schauen	look, see, gaze, behold; the looking

[Definitions continued on following pages]

1 [repeated]

Wenn aus den Weltenweiten
Die Sonne spricht zum Menschensinn
Und Freude aus den Seelentiefen
Dem Licht sich eint im Schauen,
Dann ziehen aus der Selbstheit Hülle
Gedanken in die Raumesfernen
Und binden dumpf
Des Menschen Wesen an des Geistes Sein.

When from the width of worlds
The Sun speaks to the human sense,
And joy out of the depths of soul
Unites with light in Man's beholding,
Then thoughts withdraw from Selfhood's sheath
To farthest distances of space
And dimly bind
Man's being to the Spirit's life.

dann	then
ziehen	to pull, draw from
der	the (see 'things to know')
Selbstheit	selfhood
Hülle	sheath, covering; "hull", "husk"
Gedanken	thoughts
in	in
Raumesfernen	far distances of space (space distances)
binden	bind
dumpf	dull, gloomy; dully
des	the (see 'things to know')
Menschen	human being, human beings
Wesen	essence, being
an	preposition: at,' 'on,' 'to,' 'upon,' or 'by,' variously by context
Geistes	spirit; in German it is also used more broadly in the sense of mind.
Sein	to be, being

[Definitions continued from previous pages]

2

Ins Äußre des *Sinnesalls*
Verliert Gedankenmacht ihr Eigensein,
Es finden Geisteswelten
Den *Menschensprossen wieder,*
Der *seinen Keim* in *ihnen,*
Doch seine *Seelenfrucht*
In sich *muss finden.*

Into the senses' outer world
Power of thought its separate being loses;
The worlds of Spirit find
Their human offspring once again,
And he must find his seed
In them, yet in himself
His soul's own fruit.

ins	into
Äußre	outer
Sinnesalls	sense's all, realm of perception
verliert	lose, loses, lost
Gedankenmacht	thought power
ihr	her
Eigensein	own being
es	it
finden	find; to find
Geisteswelten	spirit worlds
Menschensprossen	human shoots or sprouts, offspring
wieder	again
seinen	his
Keim	germ. Frequently translated as 'seed,' has also the sense of a bud or sprout.
ihnen	them
doch	but, yet
Seelenfrucht	soul fruit
muss	must
finden	find

3

Es spricht zum *Weltenall,*
Sich *selbst vergessend*
Und seines *Urstands eingedenk,*
Des Menschen *wachsend Ich:*
In *dir, befreiend mich*
Aus *meiner Eigenheiten Fessel,*
Ergründe ich mein *echtes* Wesen.

There speaks unto the Cosmic All,
Itself forgetting,
And mindful of its primal state,
The growing human I:
In Thee, as I set free myself
From fetters of my self-bound nature,
I find the ground of my true Being.

Weltenall	world all
selbst	one's self, self
vergessend	forgetting
Urstands	original state
eingedenk	mindful, in remembrance of
wachsend	growing, grows (like "waxing" in "waxing moon"; to grow
Ich	I
dir	you
befreiend	liberating, "freeing"
mich	me
meiner	my
Eigenheiten	peculiarity, peculiarities ("own-hood"); characreristics
Fessel	shackle; "fetter"
ergründe	explore or fathom deeply; "to plumb the depths of"
echtes	genuine

4

Ich *fühle* Wesen meines Wesens:
So spricht *Empfindung,*
Die in der *sonnerhellten Welt*
Mit Lichtesfluten sich *vereint;*
Sie will dem *Denken*
Zur *Klarheit Wärme schenken*
Und Mensch und Welt
In *Einheit fest verbinden.*

Being I feel, kin to my Being,
Thus speaketh Sentience,
Which in the sunlit world
Unites with floods of light.
To Thinking's clarity
It would give warmth,
And Man and World
Bind fast in unity.

fühle	feel, felt, to feel
so	so
Empfindung	to feel; feeling or sensation
sonnerhellten	brightened by the sun
Welt	world, worlds. Usually in broadest sense like English 'cosmos'
mit	with
Lichtesfluten	floods of light
vereint	unites
sie	you; she
will	want or intend
Denken	to think; thinking
Klarheit	clarity
Wärme	warmth
schenken	to give
Einheit	unity ("one-hood")
fest	firm; "held fast"
verbinden	connect (bind with)

5

Im Lichte *das* aus *Geistestiefen*
Im *Raume fruchtbar webend*
Der *Götter Schaffen offenbart:*
In *ihm erscheint* der *Seele* Wesen
Geweitet zu dem *Weltensein*
Und *auferstanden*
Aus *enger* Selbstheit *Innenmacht.*

Within the light that out of spirit depths
Weaves fruitfully in space,
The Gods' creative deeds revealing —
In this appears the soul's own being
Widened to Universal Life
And risen again
From narrow Selfhood's inner sway.

das	the (see 'things to know')
Geistestiefen	spirit depths
Raume	space, spaces
fruchtbar	fertile, fruitful
webend	weave, weaving
Götter	gods (understood anthroposophically as heirarchical sprital beings)
Schaffen	create; creating
offenbart	revealing; revealed, made manifest; revelation
ihm	him
erscheint	appear, appears; "shine", "scene"
Seele	soul
geweitet	expanded; "widened"
zu	to
Weltensein	world being
auferstanden	resurrected
enger	narrow
Innenmacht	inner power, inner might

6

Es *ist erstanden* aus der Eigenheit
Mein Selbst und findet sich
Als Weltenoffenbarung
In *Zeit-* und *Raumeskräften;*
Die Welt, sie *Zeigt* mir *überall*
Als *göttlich Urbild*
Des *eignen Abbilds Wahrheit.*

There has arisen from its separate state
My Self, and finds itself
As revelation of the Worlds
In pow'rs of Time and Space.
The world shows everywhere to me,
As archetype divine,
The truth of my own likeness.

ist	is
erstanden	arisen; to arise
als	as
Weltenoffenbarung	world revelation
Zeit	time
Raumeskräften	space forces
Zeigt	show
überall	everywhere ("over-all")
göttlich	divine, god-like
Urbild	archetype (primal form or image)
eignen	own
Abbilds	image (of), likeness
Wahrheit	truth

7

Mein Selbst, es *drohet* zu *entfliehen,*
Vom Weltenlichte mächtig angezogen;
Nun trete du mein *Ahnen*
In *deine Rechte kräftig ein,*
Ersetze mir des Denkens *Macht,*
Das in der *Sinne Schein*
Sich selbst verlieren will.

My Self is threatening to escape,
Unto the light of Worlds drawn mightily.
Now enter thou, my heart's Divining,
With power and strength into thy rights;
Replace the might of thinking,
That in the senses' glory
Inclines to lose itself.

drohet	threatens
entfliehen	to escape (to flee)
vom	from
Weltenlichte	world light
mächtig	mighty, powerful
angezogen	attracted to
nun	now
trete	step
du	you
Ahnen	I sense, to sense; my sensing
deine	your; yours
Rechte	right, that to which one is inherently entitled to
kräftig	powerful
ein	one, a
ersetze	replace or substitute; "to seat in place of"
Macht	power, might
Sinne	sense; senses
Schein	appearance, dazzling appearance (shine)

8

Es wächst der Sinne Macht
Im *Bunde* mit der Götter Schaffen,
Sie *drückt* des Denkens *Kraft*
Zur *Traumes Dumpfheit* mir *herab*.
Wenn göttlich Wesen
Sich meiner Seele *einen* will,
Muss *menschlich* Denken
Im *Traumessein* sich *still bescheiden*.

The senses' might now grows
In union with the Gods' creating,
It presses power of thinking
Down to the dimness of a dream.
When god-like Being
Would with my soul unite,
Then human thinking
Must humbly bide in dream existence.

Bunde	to be joined (bound) with in cooperation, as in alliance or federation
drückt	presses, suppresses
Kraft	power, powers or forces
Traumes	dream
Dumpfheit	dullness, muffled quality, vagueness
herab	(lowered) down
einen	unites; becomes one with
menschlich	human "human-like"
Traumessein	dream being
still	still
bescheiden	modestly or humbly

9

Vergessend meine *Willenseigenheit*
Erfüllet Weltenwärme sommerkündend
Mir Geist und *Seelenwesen;*
Im Licht mich zu verlieren
Gebietet mir das *Geistesschauen,*
Und kraftvoll *kündet Ahnung* mir:
Verliere *dich, um* dich zu finden.

Forgetful of my Will's own entity
The warmth of Worlds now fills
My soul and spirit, summer-heralding.
The spirit-vision bids me now
To lose myself in light;
And strongly calls my heart's Divining:
Lose thou thyself, to find thyself.

Willenseigenheit	peculiarity of will
erfüllet	fill
Weltenwärme	world warmth
sommerkündend	summer announcing; making known
Seelenwesen	soul being
gebietet	commands, to command (related to german bitte, request, and english "bid")
Geistesschauen	spirit vision (beholding, looking, gaze)
kündet	to make known
Ahnung	vision, foreboding, sensing
dich	you (reflexive)
um	in order to; nearby

10

Zu sommerlichen Höhen
Erhebt der Sonne *leuchtend* Wesen sich,
Es *nimmt* mein menschlich Fühlen
In seine *Raumesweiten* mit,
Erahnend regt im *Innern* sich
Empfindung, dumpf mir kündend,
Erkennen wirst du *einst:*
Dich fühlte *jetzt* ein *Gotteswesen.*

To lofty Summer heights
The radiant Being of the Sun arises;
It takes my human feeling
Into its own wide realms of space.
Divining, Feeling stirs
Within me, dimly warning me:
In time to come thou'lt know:
A God did feel thee then.

sommerlichen	summery (summer-like)
Höhen	heights
erhebt	rises
leuchtend	shine; shining; shines,
nimmt	takes, to take
Raumesweiten	space widths (widths of space)
erahnend	foreseeing
regt	stirs
Innern	inner
erkennen	to know, to recognize
wirst	to become
einst	once (or in indefinite future as in "some day")
jetzt	now
Gotteswesen	godly being

11

Es ist in *dieser Sonnenstunde*
An dir, die *weise Kunde* zu erkennen:
An *Weltenschönheit hingegeben,*
In dir dich fühlend zu *durchleben:*
Verlieren *kann* das Menschen-Ich
Und finden sich im Welten-Ich.

In this, the Sun's own hour, it is for thee
To recognize the tidings wisdom-filled:
To beauty of the Worlds now yielded up,
Feeling thyself in thee, experience this:
The human I can lose and find
Itself within the Cosmic I.

dieser	this; these
Sonnenstunde	sun hour
weise	wise
Kunde	knowledge
Weltenschönheit	world beauty
hingegeben	devoted, dedicated; "given over"
durchleben	live through
kann	can, able to
Menschen-Ich	human I
Welten-Ich	world I

12

Der Welten *Schönheitsglanz*
Er zwinget mich aus Seelentiefen
Des *Eigenlebens Götterkräfte*
Zum *Weltenfluge* zu *entbinden;*
Mich selber zu *verlassen,*
Vertrauend nur mich *suchend*
In Weltenlicht und Weltenwärme.

The World's fair shining glory
Constrains me from the depths of soul
To free my inner life's God-given pow'rs,
Releasing them for cosmic flight,
Forsaking Self,
And trustfully to seek myself
In light of Worlds and warmth of Worlds.

Schönheitsglanz	shine, glow of beauty
er	he
zwinget	compel
Eigenlebens	own life
Götterkräfte	godly powers (strengths, forces)
Weltenfluge	world flight
entbinden	to set free (unbind)
verlassen	leave, abandon
vertrauend	trusting
nur	only
suchend	search

13

Und *bin* ich in den *Sinneshöhen,*
So *flammt* in meinen Seelentiefen
Aus Geistes *Feuerwehen*
Der Götter *Wahrheitswort:*
In *Geistesgründen* suche *ahnend*
Dich *geistverwandt* zu finden.

When I am in the heights of sense,
Then in the depths of soul there flames
Out of the spirit-worlds of Fire
The Gods' own Word of Truth:
In grounds of spirit seek divining
To find thyself akin to spirit.

bin	Ich bin, I am; sein, to be
Sinneshöhen	sense's heights
flammt	flames, to flame
Feuerwehen	fire winds
Wahrheitswort	word of truth
Geistesgründen	spirit grounds
ahnend	divining, envisioning
geistverwandt	spirit related, spirit kindred

14

An *Sinnesoffenbarung* hingegeben
Verlor ich *Eigenwesens Trieb,*
Gedankentraum, er *schien*
Betäubend mir das Selbst zu *rauben,*
Doch *weckend nahet schon*
Im *Sinnenschein* mir *Weltendenken.*

To senses' revelation yielded up,
I lost the urge of Selfhood;
And thought-dreams, dazing me,
Seemed to deprive me of myself;
Yet waking me, draws near
In glory of the senses' Cosmic Thought.

Sinnesoffenbarung	sense's revelation
Eigenwesens	own essence, own essence's
Trieb	drive
Gedankentraum	thought dream, dream of thought
schien	seemed, appeared to
betäubend	to numb, esp. to deafen
rauben	rob
weckend	awaken
nahet	approach; approaches, comes near
schon	already
Sinnenschein	sense appearance
Weltendenken	world thinking

15

Ich fühle *wie verzaubert*
Im *Weltenschein* des Geistes Weben,
Es *hat* in *Sinnesdumpfheit*
Gehüllt mein Eigenwesen,
Zu schenken mir die Kraft,
Die *ohnmächtig* sich selbst zu *geben*
Mein Ich in seinen *Schranken* ist.

I feel the Spirit's weaving
As though enchanted in the cosmic glory,
In senses' dimness
It has enwrapped the being of my Self,
Strength to bestow on me
Which, powerless in its narrow bounds,
Mine Ego cannot give itself.

wie	like, how
verzaubert	enchanted
Weltenschein	world appearance
hat	has
Sinnesdumpfheit	sense's dullness
gehüllt	enveloped; "hull", "husk"
ohnmächtig	powerless (without power)
geben	to give
Schranken	barriers, boundaries

16

Zu bergen Geistgeschenk im Innern
Gebietet *strenge* mir mein Ahnen,
Dass reifend Gottesgaben
In *Seelengründen fruchtend*
Der Selbstheit *Früchte bringen.*

To bear in inward keeping Spirit's dower
My heart's Divining sternly bids,
That ripening, gifts of God
In depths of soul fruit-bearing,
To Selfhood fruits may bring.

bergen	to shelter, to harbor, to recover, to salvage
Geistgeschenk	spirit gift
strenge	strict
dass	that
reifend	ripe; to ripen or mature; maturing
Gottesgaben	god's gifts (god-given)
Seelengründen	soul ground; soul grounds
fruchtend	to fruit, to bear fruit
Früchte	fruits
bringen	to bring

17

Es spricht das *Weltenwort,*
Das ich *durch Sinnestore*
In Seelengründe *durfte führen:*
Erfülle deine Geistestiefen
Mit meinen Weltenweiten
Zu finden einstens mich in dir.

Thus speaks the Word of Worlds
Which I through senses' gate
Might lead into the grounds of soul:
Fill thou thy spirit depths
With all My width of worlds
To find hereafter Me in thee.

Weltenwort	world word
durch	through
Sinnestore	sense's gate
durfte	Ich durfte, I was allowed; to allow
führen	to lead

18

Kann ich die Seele *weiten,*
Dass sie sich selbst verbindet
Empfangnem Welten-Keimesworte?
Ich ahne, dass ich Kraft muss finden
Die Seele *würdig* zu *gestalten,*
Zum *Geisteskleide* sich zu *bilden.*

Can I make wide my soul
That she may bind herself
To Cosmic Seed-Word now conceived?
My heart divines that I must find the strength
My soul to fashion worthily
To form herself into the Spirit's raiment.

weiten	widen, widths
empfangnem	receive
Welten-Keimesworte	world (cosmic) seed word
würdig	worthy
gestalten	to fashion or form into shape
Geisteskleide	spirit garment, clothing, raiment
bilden	to form

19

Geheimnisvoll das *Neu-Empfang'ne*
Mit der *Erinn'rung* zu *umschließen,*
Sei meines *Strebens weitrer* Sinn:
Es *soll erstarkend Eigenkräfte*
In meinem Innern wecken
Und *werdend* mich mir selber geben.

Mysteriously with Memory to enclose
That which has newly been conceived,
This be my striving's further aim,
And growing strong, it shall awaken
Powers of Selfhood in my inward being,
And in becoming give myself to me.

geheimnisvoll	mysterious, "full of mystery"
Neu-Empfang'ne	newly received
Erinn'rung	memory
umschließen	enclose
Strebens	striving; strive
soll	should
erstarkend	strengthening, strengthen
Eigenkräfte	own powers
werdend	becoming

20

So fühl ich *erst* mein Sein,
Das *fern* vom Welten-Dasein
In sich, sich selbst *erlöschen*
Und *bauend* nur *auf* eignem *Grunde*
In sich, sich selbst *ertöten müsste.*

So now I feel my Life,
Which, severed from the Universal Being
Within itself, must quench itself,
And building merely on its own foundations
Within itself, bring death upon itself.

erst	first
fern	distant
Welten-Dasein	world existence
erlöschen	extinguish
bauend	building
auf	on, in, at
Grunde	ground
ertöten	to kill
müsste	would have to

21

Ich fühle fruchtend *fremde* Macht
Sich *stärkend* mir mich selbst *verleihn,*
Den Keim empfind ich reifend
Und Ahnung *lichtvoll* weben
Im Innern an der Selbstheit Macht.

I feel strange power bearing fruit
And gathering strength, now lend myself to me;
I sense the seed maturing,
And my Divining weave in light
Within myself at Selfhood's power.

fremde   strange, like a stranger
stärkend   strengthening
verleihn   lent, to lend
lichtvoll   full of light

22

Das Licht aus Weltenweiten,
Im Innern *lebt* es kräftig *fort,*
Es *wird* zum *Seelenlichte*
Und leuchtet in die Geistestiefen,
Um Früchte zu entbinden,
Die *Menschenselbst* aus *Weltenselbst*
Im *Zeitenlaufe* reifen *lassen.*

The Light from world-wide spaces
Lives on in me with strength,
It turns to light of soul
And shines into the depths of spirit
The fruits to liberate
Which in the course of time will ripen
The Self of Man out of the Self of Worlds.

lebt	lives
fort	onward, away
wird	becomes
Seelenlichte	soul light
Menschenselbst	human self
Weltenselbst	world self
Zeitenlaufe	course of time
lassen	let

23

Es *dämpfet herbstlich* sich
Der Sinne *Reizesstreben,*
In *Lichtesoffenbarung mischen*
Der *Nebel* dumpfe *Schleier* sich,
Ich selber schau in Raumesweiten
Des *Herbstes Weltenschlaf,*
Der *Sommer* hat an mich
Sich selber hingegeben.

Into autumnal dimness
The stirring of the senses dies away.
Dim veils of mist now mingle
With revelations of the light;
And I behold in widths of space
The Autumn's winter-sleep.
The Summer has itself
Now yielded up to me.

dämpfet	dampens
herbstlich	autumnal
Reizesstreben	striving for charm
Lichtesoffenbarung	revelation of light
mischen	mix
Nebel	fog
Schleier	veil
Herbstes	autumn
Weltenschlaf	world sleep
Sommer	summer

24

Sich selbst *erschaffend stets*
Wird *Seelensein* sich selbst *gewahr;*
Der *Weltengeist,* er strebet fort
In *Selbsterkenntnis neu belebt*
Und schafft aus *Seelenfinsternis*
Des *Selbstsinns Willensfrucht.*

Ever anew itself creating
Soul-being of itself becomes aware;
The Spirit of the World strives on
New-quickened in Man's knowledge of himself,
Creating out of darkness of the soul
What sense of Selfhood yields as fruit of Will.

erschaffend	to create; creating
stets	always
Seelensein	soul being
gewahr	aware, conscious; "wary"
Weltengeist	world spirit
Selbsterkenntnis	self-knowledge
neu	new
belebt	lively
Seelenfinsternis	soul darkness
Selbstsinns	self-sense
Willensfrucht	fruit of will

25

Ich *darf* nun mir *gehören*
Und leuchtend *breiten Innenlicht*
In Raumes- und in *Zeitenfinsternis*.
Zum *Schlafe drängt natürlich* Wesen,
Der Seele *Tiefen* sollen *wachen*
Und wachend *tragen Sonnengluten*
In *kalte Winterfluten*.

I may now to myself belong,
And radiantly spread inward light
Into the darkness of all space and time.
All natural Being presses towards sleep,
The depths of soul shall waken,
And waking carry gleams of Sun
Into cold floods of Winter.

darf	may
gehören	belong
breiten	spread
Innenlicht	inner light
Zeitenfinsternis	times of darkness
Schlafe	sleep
drängt	pushes
natürlich	naturally
Tiefen	depths, deeps
wachen	watch; watching
tragen	carry, to carry
Sonnengluten	sun glow
kalte	cold
Winterfluten	winter floods

26

Natur, dein *mütterliches* Sein,
Ich trage es in meinem *Willenswesen;*
Und meines *Willens Feuermacht,*
Sie *stählet* meines Geistes Triebe,
Dass sie *gebären Selbstgefühl,*
Zu tragen mich in mir.

Nature, I bear thy Motherhood
Within the being of my Will,
And through my Will's own Fire
My spirit's impulses are steeled
That they may bring forth feeling of the Self
To bear myself in me.

Natur	nature
mütterliches	maternal
Willenswesen	being of will
Willens	will, readiness, faculty of will
Feuermacht	fire's might
stählet	harden, to steel
gebären	give birth; "to bear"
Selbstgefühl	self-feeling

27

In meines Wesens Tiefen *dringen*
Erregt ein *ahnungsvolles Sehnen,*
Dass ich mich *selbstbetrachtend* finde
Als *Sommersonnengabe,* die als Keim
In *Herbstesstimmung wärmend* lebt
Als meiner Seele *Kräftetrieb.*

Into my being's depths to press
Stirs up a longing filled with heart's Divining
That self-observing I may find myself
As gift of Summer's Sun, which as a seed
Warmth-giving lives in autumn-mood
As bud of powers of my soul.

dringen	penetrate
erregt	excited; bestirred
ahnungsvolles	full of portent
Sehnen	to yearn
selbstbetrachtend	self-contemplating, self considering
Sommersonnengabe	gift of summer sun
Herbstesstimmung	autumn mood
wärmend	warming
Kräftetrieb	driving force

28

Ich kann im Innern neu belebt
Erfühlen eignen Wesens Weiten
Und *krafterfüllt Gedankenstrahlen*
Aus *Seelensonnenmacht*
Den *Lebensrätseln lösend spenden,*
Erfüllung manchem Wunsche leihen,
Dem *Hoffnung* schon die *Schwingen lähmte.*

I can, new-quickened in myself
Now feel the breadths of my own being,
And filled with power, shed rays of Thought
From Sun-begotten might of soul
Upon life's riddles, so unravelling them,
And grant to many a wish fulfilment
Whose wings Hope has already lamed.

erfühlen	to feel or to sense
krafterfüllt	powerful; "full of power"
Gedankenstrahlen	thought rays, thought streams
Seelensonnenmacht	soul sunlight power
Lebensrätseln	life's mysteries (riddles)
lösend	solving, solves
spenden	donate
Erfüllung	fulfillment
manchem	some
Wunsche	wish
leihen	lend
Hoffnung	hope
Schwingen	swing
lähmte	to paralyze, lame

29

Sich selbst des Denkens Leuchten
Im Innern kraftvoll zu *entfachen,*
Erlebtes sinnvoll deutend
Aus Weltengeistes *Kräftequell,*
Ist mir nun *Sommererbe*
Ist *Herbstesruhe* und *auch Winterhoffnung.*

Oneself the Light of Thinking
With power and strength to fan within,
The sense of things lived through interpreting
From the World-Spirit's Well of powers:
This is for me now Summer's heritage,
Is Autumn's calm, and also Winter's hope.

entfachen	ignite
Erlebtes	to experience
sinnvoll	meaningful ("sensible")
deutend	interpreting, signifying, indicating
Kräftequell	source of strength
Sommererbe	summer heritage
Herbstesruhe	autumn rest
auch	also
Winterhoffnung	winter hope

30

Es *sprießen* mir im *Seelensonnenlicht*
Des Denkens reife Früchte,
In *Selbstbewußtseins Sicherheit*
Verwandelt alles Fühlen sich,
Empfinden kann ich *freudevoll*
Des Herbstes *Geisterwachen,*
Der *Winter* wird in mir
Den *Seelensommer* wecken.

Within the sunlight of my soul
Spring ripened fruits of Thinking.
Into the certainty of self-awareness
All feeling now transforms itself,
And I can sense with joy
The Autumn's spirit-wakening.
The Winter will arouse in me
The Summer of the soul.

sprießen	sprout; sprouted; sprouting
Seelensonnenlicht	soul sunlight
Selbstbewußtseins	self-awareness, consciousness of self
Sicherheit	certainty, security
verwandelt	transformed
alles	all, everything
freudevoll	joyful
Geisterwachen	spirit awakening
Winter	winter
Seelensommer	soul summer

31

Das Licht aus Geistestiefen,
Nach außen strebt es *sonnenhaft,*
Es wird zur *Lebenswillenskraft*
Und leuchtet in der Sinne Dumpfheit,
Um Kräfte zu entbinden,
Die *Schaffensmächte* aus *Seelentrieben*
Im *Menschenwerke* reifen lassen.

The light from spirit depths
Strives outward like the Sun,
It turns to strength of will for living
And shines into the senses' dimness,
Forces to liberate
Which ripen from the soul's impulses
Creative powers in the work of Man.

nach	after
außen	outside, outwards
strebt	strives
sonnenhaft	sun-like
Lebenswillenskraft	life's willpower
Schaffensmächte	creative might; creative powers
Seelentrieben	soul drives
Menschenwerke	human works

32

Ich fühle fruchtend eigne Kraft
Sich stärkend mich der Welt verleihn,
Mein Eigenwesen fühl ich *kraftend*
Zur Klarheit sich zu *wenden*
Im *Lebens-Schicksalsweben*.

I feel my inborn forces bearing fruit
And gathering strength, now lend me to the world,
I feel my Selfhood charge itself with power
To turn towards clarity
In weaving of life's Destiny.

kraftend   powerful
wenden   turn, turns ("wend")
Lebens-   life's fate weaving
Schicksalsweben

33

So fühlr ich erst die Welt,
Die *außer* meiner Seele *Miterleben*
An sich nur *frostig leeres Leben*
Und *ohne* Macht sich offenbarend
In Seelen sich von neuem schaffend
In sich den *Tod* nur finden *könnte*.

So now I feel the World
Which, left without my soul's experience,
Alone would be but frozen empty life,
And Glory without Power
— Arising new in human souls —
Within itself would nothing find save death.

außer	except
Miterleben	experience, experience together
frostig	frosty
leeres	emptier; empty
Leben	life; life's
ohne	without
Tod	death
könnte	could

34

Geheimnisvoll das *Alt-Bewahrte*
Mit neu erstandnem Eigensein
Im Innern sich *belebend* fühlen:
Es soll *erweckend Weltenkräfte*
In meines Lebens *Außenwerk ergießen*
Und werdend mich ins *Dasein prägen.*

Mysteriously what has been kept of old
To feel within me, quickening
With newly risen Selfhood,
This shall in outward labour of my life,
Awakening, pour out forces of the worlds
And in becoming print me in existence.

Alt-Bewahrte	old-established
belebend	revitalizing
erweckend	awakening
Weltenkräfte	world forces
Außenwerk	it appears intended as "outer actions;" alternatively refers to outer objects such as fortifications or similar "works"
ergießen	pour, to pour out
Dasein	existence
prägen	shape, stamp, imprint, embed

35

Kann ich das Sein erkennen,
Dass es sich *wiederfindet*
Im Seelen-Schaffens-Drange?
Ich fühle, dass mir Macht verliehn
Das eigne Selbst dem Weltenselbst
Als *Glied* bescheiden *einzuleben.*

Can I true Being know
That it may find itself anew
In urge of soul's creating?
I feel that power is lent me
This Self of mine into the Self of Worlds
To live as member humbly.

wiederfindet	finds again
Seelen-Schaf-	soul-creating urge
fens-Drange	
Glied	member
einzuleben	to live into

36

In meines Wesens Tiefen spricht
Zur Offenbarung *drängend*
Geheimnisvoll das Weltenwort:
Erfülle deiner *Arbeit Ziele*
Mit meinem *Geisteslichte*
Zu *opfern* dich durch mich.

Now speaks within my being's depths
To revelation pressing
Mysteriously the Word of Worlds:
Fill thou with My spirit-light
The aims of all thy labour
To sacrifice thyself through Me.

drängend	urging
Arbeit	work
Ziele	goal, goals
Geisteslichte	spiritual light
opfern	sacrifice

37

Zu tragen *Geisteslicht* in *Weltenwinternacht*
Erstrebet selig meines *Herzens* Trieb,
Dass leuchtend *Seelenkeime*
In *Weltengründen wurzeln*
Und *Gotteswort* im *Sinnesdunkel*
Verklärend alles Sein *durchtönt.*

To carry Spirit-light into world's winter-night
Is now the blissful impulse of my heart,
That, shining, seeds of soul
Take root in grounds of World
And Word Divine in senses' gloom resound,
Transfiguring, through all that Is.

Geisteslicht	light of the spirit
Weltenwinternacht	world winter night
erstrebet	strive for
selig	blissfully, blessed
Herzens	heart's, hearts
Seelenkeime	seeds of soul
Weltengründen	world foundations
wurzeln	roots
Gotteswort	god's word
Sinnesdunkel	sensory darkness
verklärend	transfiguring, glorifying
durchtönt	resounds through

38

Ich fühle wie *entzaubert*
Das *Geisteskind* im *Seelenschoß*,
Es hat in *Herzenshelligkeit*
Gezeugt das *heilge* Weltenwort
Der Hoffnung *Himmelsfrucht*,
Die *jubelnd* wächst in *Weltenfernen*
Aus meines Wesens *Gottesgrund*.

I feel the Spirit-Child
Now conjured free within the womb of soul;
In clarity of heart
The holy Word of Worlds has now begotten
The heavenly fruit of Hope,
Which grows rejoicing into farthest worlds
Out of my being's ground divine.

entzaubert	disenchanted
Geisteskind	child of the spirit
Seelenschoß	soul's lap
Herzenshelligkeit	heart's brightness
gezeugt	begotten
heilge	holy
Himmelsfrucht	heavenly fruit
jubelnd	rejoicing
Weltenfernen	world distances
Gottesgrund	God's ground

39

An *Geistesoffenbarung* hingegeben
Gewinne ich des *Weltenwesens* Licht,
Gedankenkraft, sie wächst
Sich *klärend* mir mich selbst zu geben
Und weckend löst sich mir
Aus *Denkermacht* das Selbstgefühl.

To spirit-revelation yielded up,
I win the light of Universal Being.
Now waxes power of thought
And growing clearer, gives myself to me;
Awakening me, there springs
From Thinker's might, experience of the Self.

Geistesoffenbarung	spiritual revelation
gewinne	win
Weltenwesens	world essence
Gedankenkraft	power of thought
klärend	clarifying
Denkermacht	thinker's power

40

Und bin ich in den Geistestiefen,
Erfüllt in meinen Seelengründen
Aus Herzens *Liebewelten*
Der Eigenheiten leerer *Wahn*
Sich mit des Weltenwortes *Feuerkraft.*

When I am in the spirit depths,
Then in the grounds of soul,
Out of the heart's own world of Love
Empty illusion of my self-bound nature
Is filled with Fire of the Cosmic Word.

Liebewelten	worlds of love
Wahn	delusion
Feuerkraft	fire-power

41

Der Seele Schaffensmacht
Sie strebet aus dem *Herzensgrunde*
Im *Menschenleben* Götterkräfte
Zu rechtem *Wirken* zu *entflammen,*
Sich selber zu gestalten
In *Menschenliebe* und im Menschenwerke.

The soul's creative might
Now strives out of the heart's deep ground
To kindle to right action
Powers of Gods in life of Man,
To mould herself
In human Love and human Work.

Herzensgrunde	heart's depths
Menschenleben	human life
Wirken	to work; working
entflammen	inflame
Menschenliebe	love of humanity; human love

42

Es ist in diesem *Winterdunkel*
Die Offenbarung eigner Kraft
Der Seele *starker* Trieb,
In *Finsternisse* sie zu *lenken*
Und ahnend *vorzufühlen*
Durch *Herzenswärme* Sinnesoffenbarung.

Within this winter-gloom
The soul's impulse is strong
To manifest her proper power,
To guide herself to realms of darkness
And in divining to forefeel
Through warmth of heart the senses' revelation.

Winterdunkel	winter darkness
starker	stronger
Finsternisse	darknesses
lenken	steer
vorzufühlen	to anticipate, to feel in advance
Herzenswärme	heart's warmth

43

In *winterlichen* Tiefen
Erwarmt des Geistes *wahres* Sein,
Es *gibt* dem Weltenscheine
Durch *Herzenskräfte Daseinsmächte;*
Der *Weltenkälte trotzt* erstarkend
Das *Seelenfeuer* im *Menscheninnern.*

In wintry depths profound
The spirit's very being gathers warmth,
It gives to cosmic glory,
Through forces of the heart, the power to Be.
The fire of soul in Man
Grows stronger and defies the cosmic cold.

winterlichen	wintry
erwarmt	warmed
wahres	true
gibt	gives
Herzenskräfte	heart's forces
Daseinsmächte	forces of existence
Weltenkälte	world coldness
trotzt	defies
Seelenfeuer	soul fire
Menscheninnern	human interior, human inwardness

44

Ergreifend neue *Sinnesreize*
Erfüllet *Seelenklarheit,*
Eingedenk *vollzogner Geistgeburt,*
Verwirrend sprossend *Weltenwerden*
Mit meines Denkens *Schöpferwillen.*

Grasping new stirrings of the senses,
In mindfulness of spirit-birth achieved,
Soul-clarity now fills
Bewildering, springing growth of worlds
With the creative will of my own Thinking.

ergreifend	gripping
Sinnesreize	sensory impressions or stimuli
Seelenklarheit	soul clarity
vollzogner	completed
Geistgeburt	spiritual birth
verwirrend	confusing
Weltenwerden	world becoming
Schöpferwillen	creative will

45

Es *festigt* sich Gedankenmacht
Im Bunde mit der Geistgeburt,
Sie *hellt* der Sinne dumpfe *Reize*
Zur *vollen* Klarheit auf.
Wenn *Seelenfülle*
Sich mit dem Weltenwerden einen will,
Muss Sinnesoffenbarung
Des Denkens Licht empfangen.

The power of Thought grows firm
In union with the spirit's birth,
It lightens up dim stirrings of the senses
Into full clarity.
When soul-abundance
Would join with growth of worlds,
Then senses' revelation
Must needs receive the light of Thought.

festigt	solidifies
hellt	brightens
Reize	(sensory) charms, stimuli
vollen	full
Seelenfülle	soul fullness

46

Die Welt, sie drohet zu betäuben
Der Seele *eingeborne* Kraft;
Nun trete du, Erinnerung,
Aus Geistestiefen leuchtend auf
Und *stärke* mir das Schauen,
Das nur durch *Willenskräfte*
Sich selbst *erhalten* kann.

The World is threatening to stun
The inborn power of the soul.
Now, Memory, stand forth
Out of the depths of spirit radiantly,
And strengthen my Beholding,
Which through the power of Will alone
Can keep itself in being.

eingeborne   innate; inborn
stärke   strength
Willenskräfte   forces of will
erhalten   to receive

47

Es will erstehen aus dem *Weltenschoße,*
Den Sinnenschein *erquickend, Werdelust,*
Sie finde meines Denkens Kraft
Gerüstet durch die *Gotteskräfte*
Die kräftig mir im Innern leben.

There will arise out of the womb of Worlds
Requick'ning senses' glory, joy in growth.
Now may it find my thinking-power
Armed with the God-begotten forces,
Which live in strength within me.

Weltenschoße	world lap, ~bosom, ~womb
erquickend	refreshes; quickens
Werdelust	joy of becoming
gerüstet	equipped, armed, fortified
Gotteskräfte	God's powers, divine powers

48

Im Lichte das aus *Weltenhöhen*
Der Seele machtvoll *fließen* will
Erscheine, lösend *Seelenrätsel,*
Des Weltendenkens Sicherheit
Versammelnd seiner *Strahlen* Macht
Im *Menschenherzen Liebe* weckend.

Within the light that out of Cosmic Heights
Wills mightily to flow into my soul,
May there appear, unrav'ling riddles of soul
The certainty of Universal Thinking,
And gathering the power of its rays
Awaken Love within the human heart.

Weltenhöhen	world heights
fließen	to flow
Seelenrätsel	soul riddle
versammelnd	gathering, assembling
Strahlen	rays, beams
Menschenherzen	human hearts
Liebe	love

49

Ich fühle Kraft des Weltenseins:
So spricht *Gedankenklarheit,*
Gedenkend eignen Geistes Wachsen
In *finstern Weltennächten*
Und *neigt* dem nahen *Weltentage*
Des Innern *Hoffnungsstrahlen.*

Power I feel, of Universal Life;
Thus speaks the clarity of Thought,
Rememb'ring growth of its own spirit
Through dark nights of the world,
And bends towards th' approaching cosmic day
The inner beams of Hope.

Gedankenklarheit	clarity of thought
gedenkend	remembering; "calling to mind"
finstern	dark
Weltennächten	world nights
neigt	tends
Weltentage	world day
Hoffnungsstrahlen	rays of hope, streams of hope

50

Es spricht zum Menschen-Ich,
Sich machtvoll offenbarend
Und seines Wesens Kräfte lösend,
Des *Weltendaseins* Werdelust:
In dich mein Leben *tragend*
Aus seinem *Zauberbanne*
Erreiche ich mein wahres Ziel.

There speaks unto the human I,
Mightily itself revealing
And setting free its very powers,
The joy-in-growth of World-existence:
Into thee my life transferring
Out of the spell of its enchantment,
I reach my own true aim.

Weltendaseins   world existence
tragend   carrying
Zauberbanne   magic spells
erreiche   achieves; "reaches"

51

Ins Innre des *Menschenwesens*
Ergießt der Sinne *Reichtum* sich,
Es findet sich der Weltengeist
Im *Spiegelbild* des *Menschenauges,*
Das seine Kraft aus ihm
Sich neu erschaffen muss.

Into the inner being of Man
The riches of the senses pour themselves,
The Spirit of the World now finds Himself
In mirrored image of the human eye,
Which must itself create anew
Its power out of Him.

Menschenwesens	human nature
Reichtum	wealth, riches
Spiegelbild	mirror image
Menschenauges	human eye

52

Wenn aus den Seelentiefen
Der Geist sich wendet zu dem Weltensein
Und *Schönheit quillt* aus Raumesweiten,
Dann zieht aus *Himmelsfernen*
Des Lebens Kraft in *Menschenleiber*
Und einet, machtvoll wirkend,
Des Geistes Wesen mit dem *Menschensein.*

When from the depths of soul
The spirit turns towards the life of Worlds
And beauty wells from widths of space,
Then out of farthest heavens
The force of Life draws into human bodies
And working pow'rfully unites
The Spirit's being with the life of Man.

Schönheit	beauty
quillt	wells up
Himmelsfernen	heavenly distances
Menschenleiber	human bodies
Menschensein	being human

Alphabetic Glossary and Cross-Reference

Using the Glossary

Words with similar stems may take different forms: verbs may be conjugated variously, when used with different pronouns; noun and verb forms of the same derivation may be similar or identical; adjectives will take different endings depending on case, and so on. These words will generally be listed together to reflect their similar underlying meaning. Their form and syntactic function in each verse reference is best inferred from its context within the overall German verse. Each verse number cross reference in the third column will reference one or another form of the listed words.

The translated English verse, by no means "word for word," should be of assistance in understanding the specific usages in the *Seelenkalender*. Use of a complete German dictionary would of course be of further help, but it is expected that the meanings provided here will go a long way in developing comprehension. A particular strong reading of the verses is not intended in the definitions; sometimes alternative word-senses are provided, in other cases, more narrow meanings that fit the apparent sense are provided.

Quoted English words are generally meant to indicate common derivations with German words, as an aid to memory or understanding of etymological connections, or of related constructions. While related, they are not necessarily equivalent meanings.

The goal again is simply for the student of anthroposophy to begin to approach the German original. Many of these words have rich and complex sets of meaning associated with them; a complete study of the language would of course be necessary to achieve a full translation.

Certain ubiquitously used words, defined here, are excluded from the cross-referenced glossary: the articles *der, die, das, den, dem, des,* (the) and *ein, eines, einem, eine, einen, einer,* (a) as well as the frequently used *aus* (out, from, of), *und* (and), *in* (in), *im* (in the), *zu* (to), *zum* and *zur* (to the), and *es* (it).

Abbilds	image (of), likeness	6
ahne, Ahnen	sense, presentiment, suspecting	7, 16, 18
ahnend	divining, envisioning	13, 42
Ahnung	vision, foreboding, sensing	9, 21
ahnungsvolles	full of portent	27
alles	all, everything	30, 37
als	as	6, 27, 35
Alt-bewahrte	old-established	34
an	preposition: at,' 'on,' 'to,' 'upon,' or 'by,' variously by context	1, 11, 14, 21, 23, 33, 39
angezogen	attracted to	7
Arbeit	work	36
auch	also	29
auf	on	20, 45, 46
auferstanden	resurrected	5
außen	outside, outwards	31
Außenwerk	it appears intended as 'outer actions;' alternatively refers to outer objects such as fortifications or similar "works"	34
außer	except	33
äußre	outer	2
bauend	building	20
befreiend	liberating, "freeing"	3

belebend	revitalizing	34
belebt	lively	24, 28
bergen	to shelter, to harbor, to recover, to salvage	16
bescheiden	modestly or humbly	8, 35
betäuben, betäubend	to numb, esp. to deafen	14, 46
bilden	to form	18
bin, Sein	Ich bin, I am; sein, to be	1, 13, 20, 26, 35, 37, 40, 43
binden	bind	1
breiten	spread	25
bringen	to bring	16
Bunde	to be joined (bound) with in cooperation, as in alliance or federation	8, 45
dämpfet	dampens	23
dann	then	1, 52
darf	may	25
Dasein	existence	34
daseinsmächte	forces of existence	43
dass	that	16, 18, 26, 27, 35, 37
Denken, Denkens	to think; thinking	4, 7, 8, 29, 30, 44, 45, 47
dein, deine, deiner	your; yours	7, 17, 26, 36
Denkermacht	thinker's power	39
deutend	interpreting, signifying, indicating	29
dich	you; reflexive pronoun	9, 10, 11, 13, 36, 50
diesem, dieser	this; these	11, 42

dir	you	3, 11, 17
doch	but, yet	2, 14
drängend	urging, pressing, penetrating	36
drängt	pushes	25
dringen	penetrate, come through	27
drohet	threatens	7, 46
drückt	presses, suppresses	8
du	you	7, 10, 46
dumpf, dumpfe	dull, gloomy; dully	1, 10, 23, 45
Dumpfheit	dullness, muffled quality, vagueness	8, 31
durch	through	17, 36, 42, 43, 46, 47
durchleben	live through	11
durchtönt	resound through	37
durfte	was allowed	17
echtes	genuine	3
Eigenheit, Eigenheiten	peculiarity, peculiarities ("own-hood"); characreristics	3, 6, 40
Eigenkräfte	own powers	19
Eigenlebens	own life	12
Eigensein	own being	2, 34
Eigenwesen, Eigenwesens	own essence, own essence's	14, 15, 32
eigne, eignem, eigner, eignen	own	6, 20, 28, 32, 35, 42, 49
einen, einet	unites; becomes one with	8, 45, 52
eingeborne	innate; inborn	46
eingedenk	mindful, in remembrance of	3, 44

Einheit	unity ("one-hood")	4
einst, einstens	once (or in indefinite future as in "some day")	10, 17
eint	unites	1
einzuleben	to live into	35
empfangen, empfangnem	receive	18, 45
empfind, empfinden, Empfindung	to feel; feeling or sensation	4, 10, 21, 30
enger	narrow	5
entbinden	to set free (unbind)	12, 22, 31
entfachen	ignite	29
entflammen	inflame	41
entfliehen	to escape (to flee)	7
entzaubert	disenchanted	38
er	he	12, 14, 24
erahnend	foreseeing	10
erfühlen	to feel or to sense	28
erfülle, erfüllet, erfüllt	fill	9, 17, 36, 40, 44
Erfüllung	fulfillment	28
ergießt, ergießen	pour, to pour out	34, 51
ergreifend	gripping, seizing, grasping	44
ergründe	explore or fathom deeply;"to plumb the depths of"	3
erhalten	to receive	46
erhebt	rises	10
Erinn'rung, Erinnerung	memory	0, 19, 46
erkennen	to know, to recognize	10, 11, 35

Erlebtes	to experience	29
erlöschen	extinguish	20
erquickend	refreshes; quickens	47
erregt	excited; bestirred	27
erreiche	achieves; "reaches"	50
erschaffen, erschaffend	to create; creating	24, 51
erscheint, Erscheine	appear, appears; "shine", "scene"	5, 48
ersetze	replace or substitute; "to seat in place of"	7
erst	first	20, 33
erstanden, erstandnem, erstehen	arisen; to arise	6, 34, 47
erstarkend, erstarken	strengthening, strengthen	0, 19, 43
erstrebet	strive for	37
ertöten	to kill	20
erwarmt	warmed	43
erweckend	awakening	34
fern	distant	20
Fessel	shackle; "fetter"	3
fest	firm; "held fast"	4
festigt	solidifies	45
Feuerkraft, Feuermacht	fire-power	0, 40
	fire's might	26
Feuerwehen	fire winds	13
finde, finden, findet	find	2, 6, 9, 11, 13, 17, 18, 27, 33, 47, 51
finstern	dark	49
Finsternisse	darknesses	42
flammt, flammen	flames, to flame	0, 13

fließen	to flow	48
fort	onward, away	22, 24
fremde	strange, like a stranger	21
Freude	joy	1
freudevoll	joyful	30
frostig	frosty	33
fruchtbar	fertile, fruitful	5
Früchte	fruits	16, 22, 30
fruchtend	to fruit, to bear fruit	16, 21, 32
fühl, fühle, fühlte, fühlend, Fühlen, fühlr	feel, felt, to feel	4, 10, 11, 15, 20, 21, 30, 32, 33, 34, 35, 38, 49
führen	to lead	17
gebären	give birth; "to bear"	26
geben	to give	15, 19, 39
gebietet, gebieten	commands, to command, related to *bitte* (request - 'would you please', "bid")	0, 9, 16
Gedanken	thoughts	1
Gedankenklarheit	clarity of thought	49
Gedankenkraft	power of thought	39
Gedankenmacht	thought power	2, 45
Gedankenstrahlen	thought rays, thought streams	28
Gedankentraum	thought dream, dream of thought	14
gedenkend	remembering; "calling to mind"	49
geheimnisvoll	mysterious, "full of mystery"	19, 34, 36
gehören	belong	25
gehüllt	enveloped; "hull", "husk"	15

German	English	Pages
Geist, Geistes	spirit; in German it is also used more broadly in the sense of mind	1, 9, 13, 15, 26, 43, 49, 52
Geisterwachen	spirit awakening	30
Geistesgründen	spirit grounds	13
Geisteskind	child of the spirit	38
Geisteskleide	spirit garment, clothing, raiment	18
Geisteslicht	light of the spirit	37
Geisteslichte	spiritual light	36
Geistesoffenbarung	spiritual revelation	39
Geistesschauen	spirit vision (beholding, looking, gaze)	9
Geistestiefen	spirit depths	5, 17, 22, 31, 40, 46
Geisteswelten	spirit worlds	2
Geistgeburt	spiritual birth	44, 45
Geistgeschenk	spirit gift	16
geistverwandt	spirit related, spirit kindred	13
gerüstet	equipped, armed, fortified	47
gestalten	to fashion or form into shape	18, 41
gewahr	aware, conscious; "wary"	24
geweitet	expanded; "widened"	5
gewinne	win	39
gezeugt	begotten	38
gibt	gives	43
Glied	member	35
Götter	gods (understood anthroposophically as heirarchical spritual beings)	5, 8, 13
Götterkräfte	godly powers (strengths, forces)	12, 41

Gottesgaben	god's gifts (god-given)	16
Gottesgrund	God's ground	38
Gotteskräfte	God's powers, divine powers	47
Gotteswesen	godly being	10
Gotteswort	god's word	37
göttlich	divine, god-like	6, 8
Grunde, gründe, gründen	ground	0, 20
hat	has	15, 23, 38
heilge	holy	38
hellt	brightens	45
herab	(lowered) down	8
Herbstes	autumn	23, 30
Herbstesruhe	autumn rest	29
Herbstesstimmung	autumn mood	27
herbstlich	autumnal	23
herzen, Herzens	heart's, hearts	0, 37, 40
Herzensgrunde	heart's depths	41
Herzenshelligkeit	heart's brightness	38
Herzenskräfte	heart's forces	43
Herzenswärme	heart's warmth	42
Himmelsfernen	heavenly distances	52
Himmelsfrucht	heavenly fruit	38
hingegeben	devoted, dedicated; "given over"	11, 14, 23, 39
Hoffnung	hope	28, 38
Hoffnungsstrahlen	rays of hope, streams of hope	49
Höhen	heights	10
Hülle	sheath, covering; "hull", "husk"	1

Ich	I, (spiritual) Ego	3, 4, 13, 14, 15, 17, 18, 20, 21, 23, 25, 26, 27, 28, 30, 32, 33, 35, 38, 39, 40, 49, 50
ihm	him	5, 51
ihnen	them	2
ihr	her	2
innen, Innern, Innre	inner	0, 10, 16, 19, 21, 22, 28, 29, 34, 47, 49, 51
Innenlicht	inner light	25
Innenmacht	inner power, inner might	5
Innre	inner	51
ins	into	2, 34, 51
ist	is	6, 11, 15, 29, 42
jetzt	now	10
jubelnd	rejoicing	38
kalte	cold	25
kann, können	can, able to	0, 11, 18, 28, 30, 35, 46
Keim	germ, frequently 'seed,' has also the sense of a bud or sprout	2, 21, 27
klärend	clarifying	39
Klarheit	clarity	4, 32, 45
könnte	could	33

Kraft, *Kräfte,* *kräften*	power, powers or forces	0, 8, 15, 18, 31, 32, 42, 46, 47, 49, 50, 51, 52
kraftend	strengthening	32
Kräftequell	source of strength	29
krafterfüllt	powerful; "full of power"	28
Kräftetrieb	driving force	27
kräftig, *kraftvoll*	powerful	7, 9, 22, 29, 47
Kunde	knowledge	11
kündend, kündet	to make known	9, 10
lähmte	to paralyze, lame	28
lassen	let	22, 31
Leben, Lebens	life; life's	33, 34, 47, 50, 52
Lebens-schicksals-weben	life's fate weaving	32
Lebensrätseln	life's mysteries (riddles)	28
Lebenswillenskraft	life's willpower	31
lebt	lives	22, 27
leerer, leeres	emptier; empty	33, 40
leihen	lend	28
lenken	guide, steer	42
Leuchten, *leuchtend,* *leuchtet*	shine; shining; shines,	10, 22, 25, 29, 31, 37, 46
Licht, *Lichte,* *lichtes*	light	0, 1, 5, 9, 22, 31, 39, 45, 48
Lichtesfluten	floods of light	4
Lichtesoffenbarung	revelation of light	23
lichtvoll	full of light	21
Liebe	love	48

Liebewelten	worlds of love	40
lösend, löst	solving, solves, untangles, loosen	28, 39, 48, 50
Macht	power, might	7, 8, 21, 33, 35, 48
mächtig, machtvoll	mighty, powerful	7, 48, 50, 52
manchem	some, many	28
mein, meine, meinem, meinen, meiner, meines	my	3, 4, 6, 7, 8, 9, 10, 13, 15, 16, 17, 19, 20, 26, 27, 32, 33, 34, 36, 37, 38, 40, 44, 47, 50
Mensch, Menschen	human being, human beings	1, 3, 4
Menschen-ich	human I	11, 50
Menschenauges	human eye	51
Menschenherzen	human hearts	48
Mencheninnern	human interior, human inwardness	43
Menschenleben	human life	41
Menschenleiber	human bodies	52
Menschenliebe	love of humanity; human love	41
Menschensein	human existence	52
Menschenselbst	human self	22
Menschensinn	human senses	1
Menschensprossen	human shoots or sprouts, offspring	2
Menschenwerke	human works	31, 41
Menschenwesens	human nature	51
menschlich	human "human-like"	8, 10

mich, mir	one's self (reflexive pronoun)	3, 6, 7, 8, 9, 10, 12, 14, 15, 16, 17, 19, 21, 23, 25, 26, 27, 29, 30, 32, 34, 35, 36, 39, 46, 47
mischen	mix	23
mit	with	4, 8, 10, 17, 19, 34, 36, 40, 44, 45, 52
Miterleben	experience, experience together	33
muss	must	2, 8, 18, 45, 51
müsste	must, would have to	20
mütterliches	maternal	26
nach	after	31
nahen, nahet	approach; approaches, comes near	14, 49
Natur	nature	26
natürlich	naturally	25
Nebel	fog	23
neigt	tends, inclines	49
neu, neue, neuem	new	24, 28, 33, 34, 44, 51
Neu-empfang'ne	newly received	19
nimmt, nehmen	takes, to take	0, 10
nun	now	7, 25, 29, 46
nur	only	12, 20, 33, 46

offenbarend, *offenbart,* Offenbarung	revealing; revealed, made manifest; revelation	5, 33, 36, 42, 50
ohne	without	33
ohnmächtig	powerless (without power)	15
opfern	sacrifice	36
prägen	shape, stamp, imprint, embed	34
quillt	wells up	52
rauben	rob	14
Raume, raumes	space, spaces	5, 25
Raumesfernen	far distances of space (space distances)	1
raumeskräften	space forces	6
Raumesweiten	space widths (widths of space)	10, 23, 52
Rechte, rechten, rechtem	right, that to which one is inherently entitled to	0, 7, 41
regt	stirs	10
Reichtum	wealth, riches	51
reife, *reifen,* *reifend*	ripe; to ripen or mature; maturing	16, 21, 22, 30, 31
Reize	(sensory) charms, stimuli, excitement	45
Reizesstreben	striving (seeking) for stimulation, excitement	23
schafft, Schaffen, *schaffend*	create; creating	5, 8, 24, 33
Schaffensmacht, Schaffensmächte	creative might; creative powers	31, 41

schau, Schauen	look, see, gaze, behold; the looking	1, 23, 46
Schein	appearance, dazzling appearance (shine)	7
schenken	to give	4, 15
schien	seemed, appeared to	14
Schlafe	sleep	25
Schleier	veil	23
schon	already	14, 28
Schönheit	beauty	52
Schönheitsglanz	shine, glow of beauty	12
Schöpferwillen	creative will	44
Schranken	barriers, boundaries	15
Schwingen	swing	28
Seele, Seelen	soul	5, 8, 18, 25, 27, 33, 41, 42, 46, 48
Seelen-schaffens-drange	soul-creating urge	35
Seelenfeuer	soul fire	43
Seelenfinsternis	soul darkness	24
Seelenfrucht	soul fruit	2
Seelenfülle	soul fullness	45
Seelengründe, Seelengründen	soul ground; soul grounds	16, 17, 40
Seelenkeime	seeds of soul	37
Seelenklarheit	soul clarity	44
Seelenlichte	soul light	22
Seelenrätsel	soul riddle	48
Seelenschoß	soul's lap, ~bosom, ~womb	38
Seelensein	soul being	24
Seelensommer	soul summer	30
Seelensonnenlicht	soul sunlight	30

Seelensonnenmacht	soul sunlight power	28
Seelentiefen	soul depths	1, 12, 13, 52
Seelentrieben	soul drives	31
seelenwesen	soul being	9
Sehnen	to yearn	27
sei, Sein	to be, being	1, 19, 20, 26, 35, 37, 43
seine, seinen, seines, seinem, seiner	his	2, 3, 10, 15, 48, 50, 51
selber, Selbst	one's self, self	3, 6, 7, 12, 14, 15, 18, 19, 20, 21, 23, 24, 29, 35, 39, 41, 46
selbstbetrachtend	self-contemplating, self considering	27
Selbstbewußtseins	self-awareness, consciousness of self	30
Selbsterkenntnis	self-knowledge	24
Selbstgefühl	self-feeling	26, 39
Selbstheit	selfhood	1, 5, 16, 21
Selbstsinns	self-sense	24
selig	blissfully, blessed	37

sich	third person reflexive pronoun; himself, herself, itself	1, 2, 3, 4, 6, 7, 8, 10, 11, 15, 18, 20, 21, 23, 24, 29, 30, 32, 33, 34, 35, 39, 40, 41, 45, 46, 50, 51, 52
Sicherheit	certainty, security	30, 48
sie	you; she	4, 6, 8, 18, 26, 39, 41, 42, 45, 46, 47
Sinn, Sinne	sense; senses	7, 8, 19, 23, 31, 45, 51
Sinnenschein	sense appearance	14, 47
Sinnesalls	sense's all, realm of senses	2
Sinnesdumpfheit	sense's dullness	15
Sinnesdunkel	sensory darkness	37
Sinneshöhen	sense's heights	13
Sinnesoffenbarung	sense's revelation	14, 42, 45
Sinnesreize	sensory impressions or stimuli	44
Sinnestore	sense's gate	17
sinnvoll	meaningful, "sensible"	29
so	so	4, 13, 20, 33, 49
soll, sollen	should	19, 25, 34
Sommer	summer	23
Sommererbe	summer heritage	29
sommerkündend	summer announcing; making known	9
sommerlichen	summery (summer-like)	10

Sommersonnengabe	gift of summer sun	27
Sonne	sun	1, 10
Sonnengluten	sun glow	25
sonnenhaft	sun-like	31
Sonnenstunde	sun hour	11
sonnerhellten	brightened by the sun	4
spenden	donate, contribute	28
Spiegelbild	mirror image	51
spricht	speaks	1, 3, 4, 17, 36, 49, 50
sprießen, sprossend	sprout; sprouted; sprouting	30, 44
stählet	harden, to steel	26
stärke	strengthen	46
stärkend	strengthening	21, 32
starker	stronger	42
stets	always	24
still	silent, still	8
Strahlen	rays, beams	48
Strebens	striving	19
Strebens, strebet	striving; strive	19, 24, 41
strebt	strives	31
strenge	strict	16
suche, suchend	seek, search	12, 13
Tiefen	depths, deeps	25, 27, 36, 43
Tod	death	33
trage, tragen	carry, to carry	25, 26, 37
tragend	carrying	50
Traumes	dream	8
Traumessein	dream being	8
trete	step	7, 46
Trieb, Triebe	drive	14, 26, 37, 42

trotzt	defies, in spite of	43
überall	everywhere ("over-all")	6
um	in order to; nearby	9, 22, 31
umschließen	enclose	19
Urbild	archetype (primal form or image)	6
Urstands	original state	3
verbinden, verbindet	connect (bind with)	4, 18
vereint	unites	4
vergessend	forgetting	3, 9
verklärend	transfiguring, glorifying	37
verlassen	leave, abandon	12
verleihn, verliehn	lent, to lend	21, 32, 35
verliere, verlieren, verliert, verlor	lose, loses, lost	2, 7, 9, 11, 14
versammelnd	gathering, assembling	48
vertrauend	trusting	12
verwandelt	transformed	30
verwirrend	confusing	44
verzaubert	enchanted	15
vollen	full	45
vollzogner	completed, accomplished	44
vom, von	from	7, 20, 33
vorzufühlen	to anticipate, to feel in advance	42
wachen, wachend	watch; watching	25
wachsend, wächst, Wachsen	growing, grows (like "waxing" in "waxing moon"; to grow	3, 8, 38, 39, 49
Wahn	delusion	40
wahres	true	43, 50

Wahrheit	truth	6
Wahrheitswort	word of truth	13
Wärme	warmth	4
wärmend	warming	27
Weben, webend	weave, weaving	5, 15, 21
wecken, weckend	awaken	14, 19, 30, 39, 48
weise	wise	11
weiten, Weiten	widen, widths	18, 28
Welt, Welten	world, worlds. Usually in broadest sense like English 'cosmos'	4, 6, 12, 32, 33, 46
Welten-dasein	world existence	20
Welten-ich	world I	11
Welten-keimesworte	world (cosmic) seed word	18
Weltenall	world all	3
Weltendaseins	world existence	50
Weltendenken, Weltendenkens	world thinking	14, 48
Weltenfernen	world distances	38
Weltenfluge	world flight	12
Weltengeist, Weltengeistes	world spirit	24, 29, 51
Weltengründen	world foundations	37
Weltenhöhen	world heights	48
Weltenkälte	world coldness	43
Weltenkräfte	world forces	34
Weltenlicht, Weltenlichte	world light	7, 12
Weltennächten	world nights	49
Weltenoffenbarung	world revelation	6
Weltenschein, Weltenscheine	world appearance	15, 43
Weltenschlaf	world sleep	23
Weltenschönheit	world beauty	11

Weltenschoße	World lap, ~bosom, ~womb;	47
Weltensein, Weltenseins	world being	5, 49, 52
Weltenselbst	world self	22, 35
Weltentage	world day	49
Weltenwärme	world warmth	9, 12
Weltenweiten	world widths	1, 17, 22
Weltenwerden	world becoming	44, 45
Weltenwesens	world essence	39
Weltenwinternacht	world winter night	37
Weltenwort, Weltenwortes	world word	17, 36, 38, 40
wenden, wendet	turn, turns ("wend")	32, 52
wenn	if, when	1, 8, 45, 52
Werdelust	joy of becoming	47, 50
werdend	becoming	19, 34
Wesen, Wesens	essence, being	1, 3, 4, 5, 8, 10, 25, 27, 28, 36, 38, 50, 52
wie	like, how	15, 38
wieder	again	2
wiederfindet	finds again	35
will	want or intend	4, 7, 8, 45, 47, 48
Willens	will, readiness, faculty of will	26
Willenseigenheit	peculiarity of will	9
Willensfrucht	fruit of will	24
Willenskräfte	forces of will	46
willenswesen	being of will	26
Winter	winter	30
Winterdunkel	winter darkness	42
Winterfluten	winter floods	25

Winterhoffnung	winter hope	29
winterlichen	wintry	43
wird	becomes	22, 24, 30, 31
Wirken, wirkend	to work; working	41, 52
wirst	to become	10
Wunsche	wish	28
würdig	worthy	18
wurzeln	roots	37
Zauberbanne	magic spells	50
Zeigt	show	6
zeit	time	6
Zeitenfinsternis	darkness of time, time's of darkness	25
Zeitenlaufe	course of time	22
zieht, ziehen	to pull, draw from	1, 52
Ziel, Ziele	goal, goals	36, 50
zwinget	compel	12

www.ingramcontent.com/pod-product-compliance
Lightning Source LLC
Chambersburg PA
CBHW061809070526
44586CB00024B/2769